AF428430

The Poetry of Transcendence

copyright © 2025 Rex Bundy

Apotheosis Publications ®

Dedication

Although it is neither needed nor sought, I give all credit, honor, and gratitude to the Shekhinah, the Holy Spirit, the Ruach Ha Kodesh, who welcomes and guides all according to God's will – the all - encompassing, eternal stream of cause and effect.

Table of Contents

Forward

"The demands of the heart outweigh the intellectualism of philosophy, which strips the divine nature of all his attributes and, defining him only by that which he is not, reduces him to an 'emptiness' that is abhorrent to the Mystic poet.

In poetry, it is natural for the lover to assign personality to the beloved. In doing so, a wide range of mystical emotion is brought into play: from the loftiest abstractions and the most otherworldly passion for the infinite to the most intimate and personal realization of God, expressed in homely metaphors and religious symbols drawn indifferently from all faiths.

The language of love, which appears everywhere at a certain level of spiritual culture and which creeds and philosophies are powerless to kill, enables the fusion of those differing creeds. The poetry of mysticism might be defined on one hand as a temperamental reaction to the vision of reality; on the other hand, as a form of prophecy. As it is the special vocation of the mystical consciousness to mediate between two orders - going out in loving adoration toward God and coming home to tell the secrets of eternity to other men - so the artistic self-expression of this consciousness has a double character. It is love poetry, but love poetry that is often written with a missionary intention.

The poetry of the Mystics resolves the perpetual opposition between the personal and impersonal, the transcendent and imminent, and the static and dynamic aspects of the divine nature; between the absolute of philosophy and the 'sure true friend' of devotional religion. They have done this not by taking these apparently incompatible concepts one after the other but by ascending to a height of spiritual intuition at which they merge in the Unity and are perceived as the completing opposites of a perfect whole.

In poetry, there are no fences between the natural and supernatural worlds; everything is part of the creative play of God and, therefore, even in its humblest details, capable of revealing the player's mind.

It is by the simplest metaphors and constant appeals to needs, passions, and relations that all men understand-the bridegroom and bride, the guru and disciple, the pilgrim, the farmer-that it drives home the intense conviction of the reality of the soul's intercourse with the transcendent.

The willing acceptance of the here and now as a means of representing supernal realities is a trait common to the greatest Mystics. For them, when they have finally achieved the true theopathetic state, all aspects of the universe possess equal authority as sacramental declarations of the presence of God. Their fearless employment of homely and physical symbols, often startling and even revolting to the unaccustomed taste, is in direct proportion to the exaltation of their spiritual life.

As Ruysbroeck discerned a plane of reality upon which 'we can speak no more of Father, Son, and Holy Spirit, but only of one being, the very substance of the divine persons,' so Kabir says that 'beyond both the limited and the limitless is he, the pure being.'"

Rabindranath Tagore from his introduction to "Songs of Kabir"- 1915

The following is the poetry of mystics
from various times and religions; followed
by the account of a conversation between
Kutadanta, a Hindu Brahman, and Gotama
Siddhartha, the Buddha, taken from an early
transcription by Paul Carus (the Gospel of
Buddha -1894).

The narrative is interspersed with
commentary. I hope you find the content
useful.

The Poetry of Transcendence
with commentary

By Rex Bundy

Be utterly humble and you shall hold
to the foundation of peace.

Be at one with all living things which,
having arisen and flourished, return
to the quiet whence they came, like a
healthy growth of vegetation falling
back upon the root.

Acceptance of this return to the root
has been called quietism, acceptance
of quietism has been condemned as
fatalism.

But fatalism is acceptance of destiny
and to accept destiny is to face life
with open eyes, whereas not to accept
destiny is to face death blindfolded.

He who is open eyed is open-minded,
he who is open-minded is openhearted,
he who is openhearted is kingly,
he who is kingly is godly,
he who is godly is useful,
he who is useful is infinite
he who is infinite is immune,
he who is immune is immortal.

-Lao Tsu

In the mythos surrounding the Buddha, there is a story about his conversation with Kutadanta, the curious yet skeptical head of the Brahmans in the village of Donamati, who came to question Gotama. This tale is not dissimilar to the story of Jesus being questioned by Scribes and Pharisees attempting to discredit him.

"I am told that you are the Buddha, the holy one, the all-knowing, the Lord of the world. But if you were the Buddha, would you not come like a king in all your glory and power?" Gotama responded, "Your eyes are holden. If the eye of your mind were undimmed, you could see the glory and the power of truth."

In their efforts to convey the nature of their communion with that part of themselves that transcends the senses, teachers of the mysteries have historically been compelled to use some form of sensuous imagery, crude and inaccurate though they know such imagery to be.

Human consciousness is so entirely dependent on the senses that we find it impossible to express anything that does not arise from them. Hence the claims by these teachers that they *see* celestial light, *hear* the music of the spheres, and so on.

Kutadanta's eyes were *holden*, fixed within the egocentric self, rendering the Brahman unable to *see* anything other than a lowly monk standing before him.

Every living thing carries within itself the spark or flame of creation, the primal truth of the first vibration, the voice of God, which is the source of life itself, regardless of our situation or condition.

This was the truth to which Buddha was referring, yet Kutadanta was unable to see.

Jesus said, "I am the way, the truth, and the light.

No man comes to the Father but by me." This is a very controversial statement, a source of division and, in part, the cause of the rejection of Christianity by many over the years who see that claim as exclusionary, as elitist, and as a subtle condemnation of all other faiths. Salvation awaits those who see past the wick and wax of the candle and embrace the flame.

The Brahman continued, "Show me the truth, and I shall see it. But your doctrine is without consistency.

If it were consistent, it would stand; but as it is not, it will pass away." At that moment, Kutadanta could not grasp that doctrine may often seem to convey one message while indicating something entirely different, a signpost pointing toward a direction in which truth may be encountered, but not necessarily truth itself. The signpost may decay and eventually rust away, but the destination remains.

The Buddha replied, "The truth will never pass away."The glimpse of truth offered but not seen, the doctrinal direction expressed in Lao Tsu's poetry was:

Be at one with all living things which, having arisen and flourished, return to the quiet whence they came, like a healthy growth of vegetation falling back upon the root. Acceptance of this return to the root has been called quietism, acceptance of quietism has been condemned as fatalism. But fatalism is acceptance of destiny and to accept destiny is to face life with open eyes, whereas not to accept destiny is to face death blindfolded.

The head Brahman, clinging to self as *do* we all, was prevented from accepting that gift.

You may ask, how can this be if each of us harbors that divine flame within us? Are we not immortal? If our true nature is that flame, would we not be a part of God or even gods ourselves? Would we not go to our reward in an afterlife or reincarnate? Yet if our true nature is not that flame, what then are we?

Existence is beyond the power of
words to define: terms may be used
but are none of them absolute.

In the beginning of heaven and earth
there were no words, words came out
of the womb of matter; and whether
a man dispassionately sees to the core
of life or passionately sees the surface,
the core and the surface are
essentially the same, words making
them seem different only to express
appearance.

If name be needed, wonder names
them both: from wonder into wonder
existence opens.

-Lao Tzu

Gotama continued, "You are religious and earnest. You are seriously concerned about your soul. Yet is your work in vain because you are lacking in the one thing that is needful."

Aware that, as a Brahman, Kutadanta practiced animal sacrifice for the atonement of sins and to show reverence for the gods, the Buddha said, "Greater than the immolation of bullocks is the sacrifice of self."

Fire, air, water, and earth cannot be found outside of creation. They are the elements of creation, the components of form, but they are not the self. The twine and the wax are the components of the candle, yet only when the flame is present do we have light and warmth.

Is the self the form of the candle, the components of wick and wax? Is the self the flame, which is indistinguishable from one candle to the next? Or could the self be the momentary experience of the light and warmth of consciousness?

"Then the dust will return to the earth as it was, and the spirit will return unto God who gave it."

-Ecclesiastes 12:7. No mention of a self here. When the flame is gone, wick and wax remain. Where then is the self that we are told to sacrifice?

Indeed, Does the self even exist? The mind is a mechanism. The focal point of the incoming data imprinted upon that mind results in the creation of an ego-consciousness. The five senses, or receivers of data, converge within the blank computer mind of a human babe.

That information and experience, stemming from the universal web of cause and effect, condition the mind, and gradually, a program or reactive self-assertive ego is formed.

Think of the self as a momentary film, a bubble that temporarily separates the waters above from the waters below.

If there is no self, as this implies, perhaps the proper sacrifice is the *belief in self?* Fill a glass with water and place it in water.

There is water within and without, yet if it is given a name, you call forth the error of duality.

The Prince of the Powers of the Air, or Lucifer, has been called the father of lies. In Buddhism, this aspect of creation is called Mara, the source of illusion.

This is the firmament (Gen 1:6-8) that divides the waters from the waters, thereby fostering an appearance of separation, an appearance of one and the other; an appearance that inevitably creates a belief in an autonomous self.

The man who sees dispassionately to the core of life soon discovers the secret of existence: the truth of the non-existence of self. He sees the flame within himself and recognizes that flame within all others.

Yet, the one who sees and the one who remains blind are playing out the roles dictated by Karma, the universal flow of cause and effect. They both experience the pains and joys of existence. Kutadanta, who, despite his piety, was engrossed in samsara, was bound to the suffering and apparent isolation of the material world. The sorrow of life blinded him, so before him, he saw only a poor monk, the wick and wax only.

The universe is deathless, is
deathless because, having no finite
self, it stays infinite.

A sound man by not advancing
himself stays the further ahead of
himself, by not confining himself to
himself sustains himself outside
himself: by never being an end in
himself he endlessly becomes himself.
-Lao Tzu

The Buddha continued, "There is rebirth of character, but no transmigration of a self. Your thought forms reappear, but there is no ego entity transferred. Only through ignorance and delusion do men indulge in the dream that their souls are separate and self-existent entities.

Your heart, O Brahman, is cleaving still to self; you are anxious about heaven, but you seek the pleasures of self in heaven, and thus you cannot see the bliss of truth and the immortality of truth.

He who offers to the gods his evil desires will see the uselessness of slaughtering animals at the altar.

Blood has no cleansing power, but the eradication of lust will make the heart pure. And yet, better than worshiping gods is obedience to the laws of righteousness."

The definition of the word "lust", as used here, is not a moral judgment but rather, and more to the heart of the matter, the cleaving or attachment to material forms, including the self.

Kutadanta, being of a religious disposition and anxious about his fate after death, had sacrificed countless victims. Now he saw the folly of atonement by blood, whether animal or human.

However, not yet satisfied with the teachings of the Buddha, Kutadanta continued, "I believe, O Master, that beings are reborn, that they migrate in the evolution of life; and that, subject to the Law of Karma, we must reap what we sow. Yet you teach the non-existence of the self! Your disciples praise utter self-extinction as the highest bliss of Nirvana.

If I am merely a combination of forms, my existence will cease when I die. If I am merely a compound of sensations, ideas, and desires, where can I go at the dissolution of the body?"

Kutadanta questioned the purpose of cause and effect if indeed there was no self. Why be concerned with karma if, after death, there was no self to reap what has been sown?

daily the absolute sovereignty of cause and effect cannot help but give rise to the of free will and our understanding of the reality of self, which inevitably encompasses the nature of life and death.

Buddha answered, "Verily, I say unto you: the Blessed one has not come to teach death, but to teach life, and you do not discern the nature of living and dying."

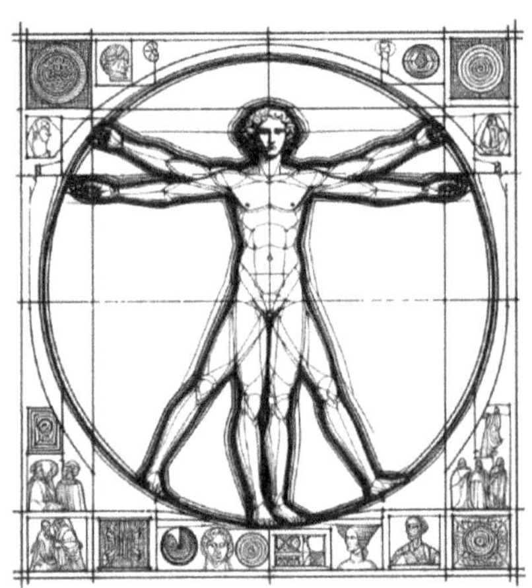

As ships are by the wind impelled,
as arrows from their bowstrings
speed, so likewise when the body
moves the windy element must lead.

Machines are geared to work by
ropes, so to this body is, in fact,
directed by a mental pull whene'er
it stand or sit or act.

No independent self is here that
could intrinsic forces prove to make
man act without a cause, to make
him stand, or walk, or move.
-Anonymous Buddhist poet

The Buddha said to Kutadanta, "Self is death and truth is life. The cleaving to self is a perpetual dying, while moving in the truth is partaking of Nirvana, which is life everlasting. This body will be dissolved, and no amount of sacrifice will save it. Therefore, seek out the life that is of the mind."

The formation of energy into clusters or compounds; birth is the only life the egocentric entity will ever experience and should be fully engaged with. But without the truth, it will be plagued by fear, anger, and lust at the prospect of that form's unforming or death.

"While contemplating the objects of the senses, a person develops attachment for them, and from such attachment, lust develops, and from lust, anger arises." - Bhagavad Gita Beyond the nonsense of "my truth" and "your truth" is the truth. Listen to me: the peace that you experience and are able to pass on to the world is directly related to the depth to which your mind rests in the truth.

This truth? It is the opposite of the lie spoken by the serpent in the garden concerning the partaking of the fruit of duality (knowledge of good and evil), "You will not die, and you can choose for yourself what is good and what is evil." The original lie of immortality and free will.

We all cohabit with a mirror that reflects the truth of self. The shunning or rejection of truth results in fear, lust, envy, and ultimately rage. The recognition of truth and the ingestion of it brings peace and ever-growing wisdom.

One mirror, one reflection with two interpretations.

One we label as demonic, the other we label Shekhinah. We have all heard the admonitions of renunciation: repent and turn away from sin, etc. We were told that this is the way to salvation or Nirvana. But, as Kabir has said, "put all imaginations away, and stand fast in that which you are."

The only true way to change your nature is to see that nature for what it is. I say that once the seeds sown by the contemplation of truth (the reality concerning the nature of self and free will) take root, those shiny objects of material existence will no longer captivate.

Experience your life with joy, knowing that those seeds planted must produce a harvest.

To what shore would you cross, oh
my heart? There is no traveler
before you, there is no road: where
is the movement, where is the rest,
on that shore? There is no water; no
boat, no boatman, is there; there is
not so much as a rope to tow the boat,
nor a man to draw it.

No earth, no sky, no time, no thing is
there: no shore, no ford! There, there
is neither body nor mind: and where
is the place that shall still the thirst of
the soul? You shall find naught in that
emptiness.

Be strong, and enter into your own
body: for there your foothold is firm.

Consider it well, oh my heart! Go not
elsewhere.
Kabir says: "put all imaginations
away, and stand fast in that which
you are."

-Kabir

Many individuals understand and believe that the initial vibration that created all things - the light and sound of God, the word spoken at the beginning - is the ultimate reality. However, the possibility of error is just a small step away.

If this word, this reality, is compared to an all-encompassing, unending ocean of life, and all things derive their being from it, it would be easy and spiritually comfortable to tell ourselves that we are drops of water within that great ocean. That we are part of God, if not gods ourselves in a way.

This ocean of life is the work of the source which we label God, but is not the source itself.

The Buddha continued, "Where self is, truth cannot be; yet when truth comes, self will disappear.

Therefore, let your mind rest in the truth; propagate the truth, put your whole will in it and let it spread. In the truth, you will live forever."

I am life, I have a voice, and my voice is life. Hearken to my voice to the exclusion of all else. This is the means by which the ground is prepared for planting.

Throughout the history of mankind there has never been a time when my presence has not been felt upon the earth.

I am the will of that which creates, I cannot be denied.

This is the seed that I plant in plain sight, invisible in its simplicity; the truth that brings peace. Accessible only through the grace that permeates and sustains all things.

Therefore, when you are called come to me quickly, for I run towards those who move towards me. Do not look to the left or the right; do not entertain vain imaginings; do not search the ends of the Earth for I stand beside you always.

-the Ruach ha-kodesh 3-4-24.

Reminding ourselves of what the Buddha previously said within the narrative, "Your heart, O Brahman, is cleaving still to self; you are anxious about an afterlife but you seek the pleasures of self in the afterlife, and thus you cannot see the bliss of truth and the immortality of truth."

The Hindu concept of Isvara is the belief in a personal Creator, but if Isvara is at the center of our belief system, we would submit unquestionably to Isvara.

We would be clay vessels formed on the potter's wheel and unable to practice independent virtuousness or evil, which would, by necessity, originate with Isvara. If the pure and the impure do not come from our Creator, then He would not be self-existent; there would be another cause besides Him.

And if, on the other hand, we adopt the belief that there is no maker and our fate is in our own hands, then there would be no initial causation. If this were the case, we would be adrift, unable to make any decision because, in order to do so, we would have to acknowledge the past experiences that weigh on that decision. We would have to re-examine the law of cause and effect, particularly the scope of its influence. Many are reluctant to do so because it leads directly to questions of self and free will.

Consider that if all things were brought into existence by choice, there would be no suffering, as no one chooses to suffer. But what of those who seem determined to suffer, those who make the same mistakes repeatedly with seemingly no concern or remembrance of the consequences? Even a child who once burned himself on a hot pot remembers the experience when confronted with a similar situation and decides not to repeat it.

Picture a man with both hands behind his back. He brings forth two closed fists and asks you to pick the one holding a coin. You pick the left, and he shows that you're wrong. He repeats the performance, and you choose the right, whereupon he opens both hands to reveal the empty. He then stands aside to show the coin lying on the floor behind him.

You might say that the man cheated; there was no possibility that you could have picked the coin. That is exactly correct; you cannot choose what you are unaware of.

And still, we cannot believe that what we perceive as free will is nothing more than conditioned reflex.

We are told by Kabir to "put all imaginations away and stand fast in that which you are."

That is the question, isn't it? What are we?

Oh friend! This body is His lyre; He
tightens its strings, and draws from
it the melody of Brahma.

If the strings snap and the keys
slacken, then to dust must this
instrument of dust return:

Kabir says: "none but Brahma can
evoke its melodies."

-Kabir

After a pause, allowing Kutadanta to fully comprehend his words, Gotama continued, "This body will be dissolved, and no amount of sacrifice will save it. Therefore, seek the life that is of the mind.

"Stand fast in that which you are."

This lyre, this form, is for the purpose of adding to the melody of God, the music of the spheres, Om(aum), Naam, the initial vibration or the flow of cause and effect.

The lyre is multifaceted (IHVH); there are layers to its existence. There is the earth, the physical body, universal matter that takes form from the air, and all this is sustained by the causal, the mercy of water granted to us by the fire contained in the word of God.

The river of Karma reacts to the cause and thereby produces the effect. By his will (cause and effect) he tightens the strings, thereby drawing forth the melody, and the song goes on.

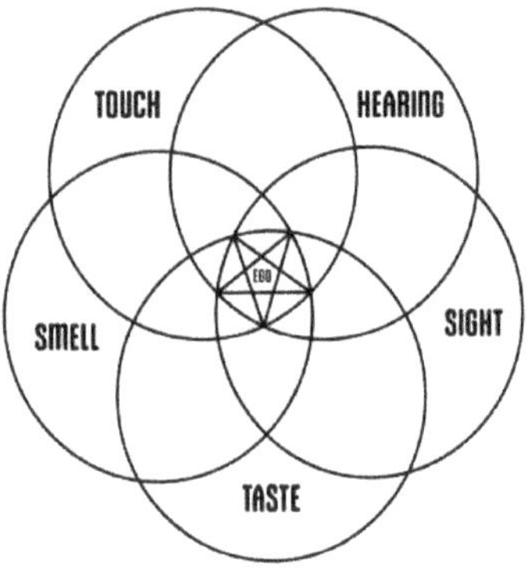

TOUCH
HEARING
SMELL
SIGHT
EGO
TASTE

**Faithful hope is dashed upon the
rocks of the mountain of truth, at
whose summit lies the floodgates of
wisdom and despair. Wisdom
comes from hearing the truth.
Despair? The same!**

-Rex Bundy

Kutadanta said, "Where, O venerable master, is Nirvana?"

"Nirvana is wherever the precepts are obeyed," replied the Buddha.

"Do I understand you rightly," questioned the Brahman, "that Nirvana is not a place, and being nowhere, it is without reality?"

"You do not understand me rightly," rejoined Gotama. "Now listen and answer these questions: where does the wind dwell?"
"Nowhere," was the reply.

Gotama retorted, "Then, Sir, there is no such thing as wind."

Kutadanta was silent, and the Buddha asked again, "Answer me, O Brahman, where does wisdom dwell? Is wisdom a locality?" "Wisdom has no allotted dwelling place," was the reply.

Said the Buddha, "Do you mean that there is no wisdom, no enlightenment, no righteousness, and no salvation because Nirvana is not a locality?"

Said Kutadanta, "I feel, O Lord, that you proclaim a great doctrine, but I cannot grasp it. Forbear with me that I ask again: tell me, O Lord, if there is no Atman (self), how can there be immortality? The activity of the mind passes, and our thoughts are gone when we have finished thinking."

Tell me, Brother, how can I renounce Maya?
When I gave up the tying of ribbons,
still I tied my garment about me:
When I gave up tying my garment,
still I covered my body in its folds.
So, when I give up passion,
I see that anger remains;
And when I renounce anger,
greed is with me still;
And when greed is vanquished,
pride and vainglory remain;
When the mind is detached and casts Maya
away, still it clings to the letter.
Kabir says, "Listen to me, dear sadhu!
The true path is rarely found."

-*Kabir*

Buddha replied: "Our thinking is gone, but our thoughts continue. Reasoning ceases, but knowledge remains."
Said Kutadanta: "How is that? Is not reasoning and knowledge the same?"

"I think, therefore I am!" is the concept behind the Brahmans' faulty thought process.

This level of resolute blindness indicates a fear of the truth so profound that we have built entire philosophies, religions, and belief systems around a lie, even as we are told it's a lie by those very systems. Was it not the serpent in the garden who told us through Eve that we would not die, and we have choice?"

The Blessed One explained the distinction by an illustration: "It is as when a man wants, during the night, to send a letter, and, after having his clerk called, has a lamp lit and gets the letter written. Then, when that has been done, he extinguishes the lamp. But though the writing has been finished and the light has been put out, the letter is still there. Thus does reasoning cease and knowledge remain; and in the same way, mental activity ceases, but experience, wisdom, and all the fruits of our acts endure."

In his poem, Kabir points out that the deeply ingrained survival instinct renders our attempts to free ourselves from illusion impotent. Even in our meditations, we reach a point where we believe that thought is suspended but soon come to realize that we are watching from outside this phenomenon, thinking about how we are not thinking.

O servant, where dost thou seek me? Lo! I am beside thee.

I am neither in Temple nor in mosque: I am neither in Kaaba nor in Kailash: neither am I in rites and ceremonies, nor in yoga and renunciation.

If thou art a true seeker, thou shalt at once see me: thou shalt meet Me in a moment of time. Kabir says, "o sadhu! God is the breath of all breath."

-Kabir

The path to liberation is invisible in its simplicity.

Repeating the Buddha yet again: "Therefore, seek the life that is of the mind. Where self is, truth cannot be; yet when truth comes, self will disappear. Let your mind rest in truth; propagate the truth, put your whole will into it, and let it spread. In the truth, you will live forever.

The cleaving to self is a perpetual dying, while <u>moving</u> in the truth is partaking of Nirvana, which is life everlasting."

Moving in the truth means experiencing your life day to day while contemplating the absolute sovereignty of cause and effect and the illusion of free will.

It has been suggested by one of my editors that perhaps I should establish a better understanding of cause and effect and why it is absolutely sovereign.

In addressing this, it must be pointed out that recognizing cause and effect's absolute sovereignty is not the goal. Even the eventual realization of the illusion of free will resulting from our reflection on this truth is not the end of our journey; it's the beginning.

While it eventually delivers us to the edge of the abyss, the daily contemplation of this truth leads toward a state of awe and reverence for creation as a whole, which will enable us to successfully traverse this wilderness in which prophets are formed.

"Awe is the feeling of being in the presence of something vast or beyond human scale that transcends our current understanding of things." - Dr.

Dacher Keltner, Professor of Psychology and head of UC Berkeley's Social Interaction Lab.

As a psychologist, Dr. Dacher, in studying human emotion, made a "deeply personal" inquiry into the elusive emotion of awe. In doing so, he discovered "how awe can transform our brains and bodies."

In his 2023 book, "Awe," he documents his work alongside his inquiries into the meaning and influence of awe throughout our history and culture. He contends that embracing awe in our lives can "put us in touch with the most human aspects of our human nature." With no mention of God or any indication toward the spiritual, he maintains a purely scientific or humanist view. As a scientist, he's bound to objective facts regardless of his personal beliefs.

Therefore, the conclusions of his published works do not transcend the individual experience and observations of the egocentric self. Hence, the study of his work cannot recognize the similarity between the emotion of awe and prayer except by inference.

To facilitate this in my own life, there is a prayer I recite to myself every morning:

"Father of all things, holy and unknowable is thy true Name. Thy will is absolute; it cannot be denied. And so, I ask for nothing, but instead give thanks for the opportunity to experience the glorious unfolding of thy will for one more day."

Again, the peace that you experience and are able to pass on to the world is directly related to the depth to which your mind rests in the truth.

Kutadanta said: "Tell me, O Lord, pray tell me, where, if the sankharas (mental impressions and forms that constitute the individual) are dissolved, is the identity of myself? If my thoughts transfer and my soul migrates, then my thoughts cease to be my thoughts, and my soul ceases to be my soul. Give me an illustration, but pray, O Lord, tell me, where is the identity of myself?"

Don't regret the past;
release your worries
about the future.
Don't think about yourself —
and stop trying not to!
Now's the time
to leave the shore
the Ocean of Unity
is calling
don't listen
don't see
don't say
don't think
don't be
JUST STOP.

-Baba Afdal Kashani

Gotama asked, "Suppose a man were to light a lamp; would it burn the night through?"

"Yes, it might do so." was the reply.

"Now, is it the same flame that burns in the first watch of the night as in the second?"

Kutadanta hesitated. He thought, "Yes, it is the same flame." But fearing the complications of a hidden meaning, and trying to be exact, he said, "No, it is not."

"Then," continued the Buddha, "are there different flames, one in the first watch and another in the second watch?" "No, sir," said Kutadanta. "In one sense it is not the same flame, but in another sense it is the same flame.

It burns the same kind of oil, it emits the same kind of light, and it serves the same purpose."

"Very well," said the Buddha, "Would you call those flames the same that have burned yesterday and are burning now in the same lamp, filled with the same kind of oil, illuminating the same room?" "They may have been extinguished during the night," suggested Kutadanta.

Said the Blessed One: "Suppose the flame of the first watch had been extinguished during the second watch.

Would you call it the same if it burns again in the third watch?" Replied Kutadanta: "In one sense, it is a different flame; in another, it is not."

The Tathagata asked again: "Does the time that elapsed during the extinction of the flame have anything to do with its identity or non-identity?"

No, sir," said the Brahman, "it does not. There is a difference and an identity, whether many years elapsed or only one second, and also whether the lamp has been extinguished in the meantime or not."

"Well, then, we agree that the flame of today is in a certain sense the same as the flame of yesterday, and in another sense, it is different at every moment.

Moreover, the flames of the same kind, illuminating with equal power the same kind of rooms, are in a certain sense the same?" The Brahman replied, "Yes, sir."

Gotama continued: "Now, suppose there is a man who feels like you, thinks like you, and acts like you; is he not the same man as you?" "No, sir," was the reply.

Said the Buddha: "Do you deny that the same logic holds true for you that holds true for the things of the world?"Kutadanta thought for a moment and rejoined slowly:

"No, I do not. The same logic holds true universally; but there is a peculiarity about myself that renders it altogether different from anything else and also from other selves. There may be another man who feels exactly like me, thinks like me, and acts like me; suppose even he had the same name and the same kind of possessions, he would not be myself."

"True, Kutadanta," answered Buddha, "he would not be you. Now, tell me, is the person who goes to school one, and that same person when he has finished his schooling another? Is it one who commits a crime, and another who is punished by having his hands and feet cut off?" "They are the same," was the reply.

"Then sameness is constituted by continuity only?" asked the Tathagata.

"Not only by continuity," said Kutadanta, "but also and mainly by identity of character."

"Very well," concluded Gotama, "then you agree that persons can be the same, in the same sense as two flames of the same kind are called the same; and you must then recognize that in this sense another man of the same character and product of the same karma is the same as you?" "Well, I do," said the Brahman.

The Buddha continued: "And in this same sense alone are you the same today as yesterday? Your nature is not constituted by the matter of which your body consists, but by your sankharas, the forms of the body, sensations, and thoughts.

Your person is the combination of the sankharas.

Whatever they are, you are. Wherever they go, you go.

Thus you will recognize in a certain sense an identity of yourself, and in another sense a difference.

But he who does not recognize the identity should deny all identity and should say that the questioner is no longer the same person as he who a minute later receives the answer.

Now consider the continuation of your personality, which is preserved in your karma. Do you call it death and annihilation, or life and continued life?"

In this way, Kutadanta was gently led to the edge of the abyss, the wilderness in which the prophets are formed.

Aleister Crowley described this place in his work, "The Wake World": "But the real serious difficulty is the outdoors. You have to leave the house of love, as they call the fourth house. You are quite, quite naked: you must take off your husband clothes, and your baby clothes, and all your pleasure clothes, and your skin, and your flesh, and your bones; every one of them must come right off. And then you must take off your feeling clothes; and then your idea clothes; and then what we call your tendency clothes which you have always worn, and which make you what you are. After that you take off your consciousness clothes, which you have always thought were your very own self, and leap out into the cold Abyss."

It is not a physical place, but an astral or mental one. A place of isolation and desolation; a place of contemplation and revelation. To see the face of God is to die. This is where the broken and desperate ego goes to seek its death in God.

There, you are faced with the truth: the non-existence of self and the absolute sovereignty of cause and effect, which eventually dissipates the illusion of free will.

I am sent to Nineveh, and I don't
want to go! Man is born, and so
must die, but he need not face it.
Denial is not a river in Egypt, the
unavoidable can be dealt with. There
are alternatives to the truth of
nonexistence, you need not face it.

The comforting appearance of
continuation can be easily realized
by the adoption of the construct of
an afterlife; whether it be heaven,
merging with the universe, entering
another dimension, reincarnation,
or some other human invention.

It is said that all roads lead to the
top of the mountain, some just go
the long way around. Likewise there
are ships that go in directions other
than Nineveh, but in all of these the
great fish awaits at journeys end. No
man fears the unavoidable, all men
fear nonexistence.

In the process of awakening I felt
abandoned, yet I clung desperately
to the belief that something was there,
just on the other side of my
abandonment. No matter what the
evidence told me I believed that I
would continue, I would pass through
the wilderness and gain my reward.

Yet, in the Abyss there is no Creator to be seen, he is beyond a veil, indeed there is no longer so much as a veil. Did you think I was afraid of the pain, afraid of physical death? These are merely unavoidable, they can be dealt with, just as a shining beacon midst the darkest of nights upon the ocean provides a straw for the drowning man.

I am left alone with the terrible truth and my doubt; and, what is this truth? That I am, and always have been nonexistent; an illusion? Fading sunlight upon a blade of grass? The premeditated result of the alchemy of the fourfold name? The serpent, himself having no choice, has divided the waters, has divided me. To what purpose? Faced now with inescapable truth, the absolute sovereignty of cause-and-effect, the self confronts the fears embedded in its own nature. To the individual whom the seeds of the Shekhinah have taken root and is delivered to Tipheret, the motivations of the Ruach ha-kodesh become clear. He finds peace and gladly makes the journey to Nineveh. He becomes a boon and teacher to mankind. But the path is narrow, like walking the edge of a straight razor.

One need not face nonexistence, the
unavoidable can be dealt with; but
keep in mind that one step to the left
or the right of the truth and that
individual is lost. His life is consumed
with rage and anger. Observe the
condition of the world left to those
who merely sense their perceived
abandonment.

-*Rex Bundy*

"I call it life and continued life," rejoined Kutadanta, "for it is the continuation of my existence, but I do not care for that kind of continuation. All I care for is the continuation of self in the other sense, which makes every man, whether identical with me or not, an altogether different person."

"Very well," said Buddha, "this is what you desire, and this is the cleaving to self. This is your error.

All compound things are transitory: they grow and decay. All compound things are subject to pain: they will be separated from what they love and joined to what they abhor. All compound things lack a self, an atman, an ego."

"How is that?" asked Kutadanta.

Like a fish knows only water, we know the phenomena of existence only through our five senses.

Kutadanta realized the truth intellectually but still could not accept it as sovereign law. It not only went against his survival instinct but also contradicted everything he had learned and experienced throughout his life, especially concerning his religion.

Because of the limitations of our senses, we experience a fraction of what exists around us, and as a result, reality cannot be fully grasped through them. The human ear, for instance, can only discern frequencies between 20 and 20,000 Hz. The range of human vision spans from 40 to 790 terahertz.

Anything outside these ranges is indiscernible, essentially invisible or inaudible.

Learning about the world under these conditions is very much like viewing a small section of a fractal image.

What we see is confusing, disjointed, and chaotic. It's only when we see a larger section that we recognize symmetry, design, and order.

Who are you, and whence do you come?
Where dwells that Supreme Spirit, and
how does He have His sport with
all created things?
The fire is in the wood; but who
awakens it suddenly? Then it
turns to ashes, and where goes the
force of the fire?
The true guru teaches that He has
neither limit nor infinitude.
Kabir says: "Brahma suits His language
to the understanding of his hearer."

-Kabir

"Where is your self?" asked the Buddha. And when Kutadanta made no reply, he continued: "The self to which you cling is in constant change. Years ago you were a small babe; then you were a boy; then a youth, and now you are a man. Is there any identity between the babe and the man?

There is an identity in a certain sense only. Indeed, there is more identity between the flames of the first and the third watch, even though the lamp might have been extinguished during the second watch. Now, which is your true self: that of yesterday, that of today, or that of tomorrow, for the preservation of which you clamor?"

Kutadanta was bewildered. "Lord of the world," he said, "I see my error, but I am still confused."

Gotama continued: "It is by a process of evolution that sankharas come to be. There is no sankhara that has sprung into being without a gradual becoming. Your sankharas are the product of your deeds in former existences. The combination of your sankharas is your self.

Wherever they are impressed, there your self migrates. In your sankharas you will continue to live, and you will reap in future existences the harvest sown now and in the past."

Only through ignorance and delusion do men indulge in the dream that their souls are separate and self-existent entities. The Buddha taught that there is no

transmigration of a self after death. What continues
are our thoughts, words, and deeds, because they
contribute to the flow of Karma, or cause and effect.

The Buddha concluded, "Dismiss the error of self, and
if there is no self, there can be no afterlife of a self.
But since there are deeds, and since deeds continue,
be careful with your deeds."

Through your thoughts, words, and deeds, become a
boon to mankind. Only one who has planted a tree,
knowing he will never sit in its shade, understands.

The secret is revealed
In quiet solitude
It is not given
But becomes self-evident
As the layers of knowledge peel back
Until nothing remains
-Curtis Church

"Verily, O Lord," rejoined Kutadanta, "this is not a fair retribution. I cannot recognize the justice that others after me will reap what I am sowing now."

The Blessed One waited a moment and then replied: "Is all teaching in vain? Do you not understand that those others are you yourself? You yourself will reap what you sow, not others."

Which do we choose: the gift or the giver? Are we going to insist on our individual reality separate from creation, or are we going to accept that we are part of it? Accept that the self is Mara, Lucifer, the bubbles' momentary film of illusion that separates the water from the water?

Kutadanta found it impossible to free his thinking from everything he had believed to be true.

"Because narrow is the gate and difficult is the way which leads to life, and there are few who find it."
-Matthew 7:14

Buddha continued, "Think of a man who is ill-bred and destitute, suffering from the wretchedness of his condition. As a boy, he was slothful and indolent, and when he grew up, he had not learned a craft to earn a living. Would you say his misery is not the product of his own actions because the adult is no longer the same person as the boy?

Verily, I say unto you: not in the heavens, not in the midst of the sea, not if you hide yourself away in the clefts of the mountains, will you find a place where you can escape the fruit of your evil actions.

At the same time, you are sure to receive the blessings of your good actions.

The man who has long been traveling and who returns home in safety is welcomed by kinfolk, friends, and acquaintances. So, the fruits of his good works bid him welcome who has walked in the path of righteousness, when he passes over from the present life into the hereafter."

Gotama reiterates one more time the non-existence of self and the absolute sovereignty of cause and effect; the truth that our thoughts, words, and deeds endure and have their continuance in the eternal flow of Karma.

"She standeth in the top of the high places. By the way in the places of the paths. She crieth at the gates, at the coming in at the doors. Council is mine, and sound wisdom: I am Binah; Unto you, O men, I call; and my voice is to the sons of man.

Now therefore hearken unto me, O ye children: for blessed are they that keep my ways. Hear instruction and be wise, and refuse it not.

Blessed is the man that heareth me, watching daily at my gates, waiting at the posts of my doors."

-Proverbs 8:2-34

Kutadanta said: "I have faith in the glory and excellency of your doctrines. My eye cannot as yet endure the light; but I now understand that there is no self, and the truth dawns upon me. Sacrifices cannot save, and invocations are idle talk. But how shall I find the path to life everlasting? I know all the Vedas by heart and have not found the truth."

"Be admonished, of making many books there is no end; and much study is a weariness to the flesh."
-Ecclesiastes 12:12

 Earlier, Kabir expressed this in a poem: "If thou art a true seeker, thou shalt at once see me; thou shalt meet Me in a moment of time," indicating how very close enlightenment is. Add to this the words of the Shekhinah: "I run towards those who move towards me."

Kutadanta was now ready to be taught.

Said the Buddha: "Learning is a good thing; but it availeth not. True wisdom can be acquired by practice only. Practice the truth that your brother is the same as you. Walk in the noble path of righteousness, and you will understand that while there is death in self, there is immortality in truth."

Moving in the truth and partaking of Nirvana, which is life everlasting, consists of experiencing your life day to day while contemplating the absolute sovereignty of cause and effect and the illusion of free will.

In Mark 12:28-34, A teacher of the law asked Jesus, "Of all the commandments, which one is the most important?"

Jesus answered, "The most important one is to love the Lord your God with all your heart, and with all your soul, and with all your mind, and with all your strength. The second is to love your neighbor as yourself."

The teacher of the law replied, "Well said, Rabbi." Jesus, seeing that the man answered wisely, said, "You are not far from the Kingdom of God."

Nirvana, the Kingdom of God, the peace and wisdom of truth, is but a breath away. Directing your attention away from self and viewing your neighbor as yourself; this is the key, the ultimate meaning of the Path of Water.

When asked by a student why human beings existed, Pythagoras said, "To observe the heavens." He wasn't referring to the mere study of stars; he was speaking of the emotion of awe, the essence of true worship. He was acknowledging the unseen source, the unnamed God of the desert, and the denial of self.

Could this be man's sole purpose, being allowed to witness the mystery of the unfolding of what we call the will of God?

O Friend! Hope for Him whilst you live, know whilst you live, understand whilst you live: for in life deliverance abides.

If your bonds be not broken whilst living,

what hope of deliverance in death? It is but an empty dream, that the soul shall have union with Him because it has passed from the body: If He is found now, He is found then.

If not, we do but go to dwell in the City of Death.

If you have union now, you shall have it hereafter.

Bathe in the truth, know the true guru, have faith in the true Name! Kabir says: "It is the spirit of the quest which helps; I am the slave of the spirit of the quest."

-Kabir

I am one
Who eats his breakfast,
Gazing at the morning-glories.

-*Matsuo Basho*